Disclaimer

Ajatshatru Sharma, © 2019 – All Rights Reserved

© Ajatshatru Sharma, 2019

No part of this e-book may be reproduced, stored, or transmitted in any form or by any means including mechanical or electronic without prior written permission from the author.

While the author has made every effort to ensure that the ideas, statistics, and information presented in this eBook are accurate to the best of his/her abilities, any implications direct, derived, or perceived, should only be used at the reader's discretion. The author cannot be held responsible for any personal or commercial damage arising from communication, application, or misinterpretation of information presented herein.

All Rights Reserved.

Contents

Disclaimer 2

Acknowledgements 6

INTRODUCTION... 7

Chapter 1: The Basics of Productivity 9

   1. What Is Productivity?... 9

   2. Why Does It Matter?... 10

   3. The Many Variables the Influence Your Bottom Line 12

      1. The Finances 13

      2. The People 13

      3. The Consumers 14

      4. The Production.. 15

   The Bottom Line 16

Chapter 2: The Game Plan: How to Be Productive from the Get Go? 18

   1. What Should You Visualize to Secure a Stable Bottom Line? 19

   2. What's on Your Game Plan? 20

      1. The Purpose: 20

      2. The Goals: 22

      3. Tools:... 23

      4. Budget:... 24

      4. Deadline:.. 24

   3. The Money Matters You Must Consider 26

      1. Setting Boundaries... 26

      2. The Overhead Expenses... 27

   The Bottom Line 30

Chapter 3: The Management: Are Your Managers Doing Their Job? 32

1. What Role Does Management Play Here?......................................33
2. A Manager's Dos and Don'ts..35
    1. Steer Clear from Micromanaging...35
    2. Keep the Door Open 36
    3. Evaluate, Asses and Comment..38
    4. Set Tangible Goals...39
    5. Discussions Come Before Repercussions 41
2. Why Is Authentic Leadership the Answer? 42
    1. Clearer Vision...44
    2. Higher Engagement 44
    3. Honest Opinions 45
The Bottom Line 46

Chapter 4: The Workforce: Is Your Work Environment Build for Productivity?..48
1. How Does Corporate Culture Affect Productivity? 51
    1. Absenteeism 52
    2. Job Stress 53
    3. Physical Environment..55
    4. Employee's Health 57
2. How Do You Judge Your Team's Contributions?...........................59
    1. Create Evaluation Forms...60
    2. Performance Measurements 61
    3. Establish Guidelines for Feedback 63
    4. Creating a Schedule 65
The Aftermath: Will Your Employees Take the Evaluations Seriously? 66
    1. The Training Sessions..70

2. The Streamline Process..71

3. The Pat on the Back and Perks..72

The Bottom Line 73

Chapter 5: The Strategies: What Can You Do to Boost Productivity?.....75

1. The Flaw in the Plan..77

2. What Is Strategic-Operational Alignment? 81

3. The Crossroads: How Do You Align Strategies with Operations? ...83

1. Planning the Perfect Alignment Strategy: What Should You Consider? 83

2. Filling in the Communication Gaps: How to Keep Everyone in the Loop? 85

3. Seeking Help from Technology: Is Software Automation the Answer? 90

The Bottom Line 96

Chapter 6: The Tech Support: Is Technology Your Biggest Asset?.........98

1. How Is Technology Supporting Your Business? 99

1. Cloud Computing 99

2. Mobile Solutions 102

3. Extreme Customer Segmentation.................................104

2. What Is the Overall Outcome?...108

1. Connectivity: 108

2. Social Impact..109

The Bottom Line 110

Parting Words 111

About Ccerebrate Business Consulting..112

Acknowledgements

This book is dedicated to everyone who has played a role in the growth and development of Ccerebrate Business Consulting. From managers, employees, customers to other professionals who have worked with us– We wouldn't have succeeded without your support.

On the personal front, this business would be just a dream if it weren't for the blessings and encouragement provided by my mother. She was the first person to believe in me and continues to do so in the present.

I wouldn't be where I am without her blessing!

-Ajatshatru Sharma

INTRODUCTION

Did you know that the term bottom line has been the bone of contention in boardrooms across the world?

In fact, our experience tells us that business meetings heat up as soon as someone brings up the subject of 'bottom line' to the table. The reason behind this is the fact that nobody wants to be held responsible for the fluctuating net incomes. So they all end up playing the blame game as the authorities try to figure out what's causing the decline.

Is there a way to find out the culprit?

Yes, there is!

However, a better way to improve your bottom line is through productivity. And in order to do that, you'll have to dig deep within the intricate workings of the company. This includes a proper evaluation of all sectors that are involved in the company's outcomes. While doing this your aim is to assess how productive and proactive your staff is. Plus, you have to reconstruct the strategies that may be able to boost your sales and increase your end-of-the-year earnings.

This isn't an easy feat to accomplish and that's where we come in. As consultants, we know how to detect and uncover the problems buried within the system. Moreover, we know how to look beyond the imminent bottom line and secure steady financial benefits for the future.

So it's safe to assume that we know a thing or two about the delicate relationship between productivity and bottom lines. That's primarily why we decided to write this book for you.

What's the purpose of this book?

In this book, we will be considering what productivity really means and how it is measured in the workplace. Moreover, this book will shed light on the various sectors within your business that have a major impact on your net income. On the whole, we want to learn a cost-effective method to tackle the many hurdles your business comes across when you run after the elusive bottom line.

So are you ready to get enlightened?

Let's get started!

Chapter 1: The Basics of Productivity

1. What Is Productivity?

In simple terms, productivity is considered to be the measurement of how efficiently you can convert your input (resources) into rewarding output. In the business world, we think of it as a general concept that related raw materials, manpower, and time to the end result. In our case, we'll specifically be looking at how much time and manual labor does it take for you to get things done?

Moreover, in order to get an estimate of your company's productivity level, you should be asking questions like:

- How many hours did it take for your team to submit a project?
- Are the deadlines being met?
- Is the work your team put in delivering satisfactory results?
- Is your efficiency being hindered by internal mismanagement?

On the whole, you'll have to analyze how your business' growth and its sales can have a maximum impact on the industry. The answer lies in the level of productivity that you've been achieving up until now and how much more productive can you become in the future. This will ensure that you get the most out of the huge efforts you put in the company.

Of course, capital, resources, energy etc does come in the mix. But our experience has shown us that in most circumstances managing the team means winning half the battle.

2. Why Does It Matter?

You may have thought that productivity could only be associated with a single person or in terms of products being manufactured in the factory. If you think like this, then you are simply looking at the minute details. In reality, it would be better for you to discard this narrow point of view and see the business as a whole.

We want you to take into consideration the way that things work around the office. While doing so, highlight the areas and aspects that might be bringing you down. This could be anything from disgruntled employees, problematic managers to malfunctioning machines. Whatever the reason might be, it's your responsibility to recognize all the places that require immediate attention. You see, smoothing these wrinkles out will let you have a head start on changing the methodology of how the company functions.

This might seem pretty ordinary to you right now.

Many of you might be wondering why we are going over seemingly basic stuff that you already know about. The thing is that a vast majority of businessmen are under the impression that the more they work the better results they'll get.

While this may hold true for some business plans, it isn't exactly a common occurrence for most. That's because sometimes you are still left with nothing despite the demanding assignments and mandatory overtimes you set for your team. The reason is that all the work is going to waste because the inputs aren't being able to generate the kind of outputs and sales that you envisioned.

In other words, more work doesn't necessarily create more profit. This is where enhancing the company's productivity can flip the scene. That's because working towards better productivity allows you to get your priorities straightened out. Not only will this boost your revenue. But it will also effectively lower the cost taken to achieve that target as well.

More importantly, strategic planning can help eliminate wastage of time and resources that take place on a daily basis. All of this will lead to a bigger bottom line that secures consistent revenue during the year. In short, productivity isn't *merely* a buzzword. It's an actual stance that businesses should take if they wish to work towards long-term outcomes. But before we divulge deeper into this proactive game plan, you must understand how the various factors come into play.

3. The Many Variables the Influence Your Bottom Line

In case you haven't figured it out yet, productivity has a major influence on your bottom line. But it's not just one single thing that sets the momentum. Rather it is a million different things that combine to form your net incomes.

Here are a few factors that determine your bottom line:

1. The Finances

It's hardly a secret that your budget is chiefly responsible for the kind of products and the quality of work you produce. After all, business is all about money and these matters are the "sensitive issues" in every meeting you conduct.

The thing is that almost 30% of new startups fail because they have no idea how to utilize their money in the right direction. Hence, they end up squandering and exhausting all the funds they had after gaining the approval of banks and benefactors.

How can you solve this problem? The key is to invest in the necessities and commodities that enhance productivity. This means no more purchases being made solely on the basis of appearance or popularity. We will discuss this matter further in the book when we talk about a productive business plan.

2. The People

Who are these people that hold back your business? These nameless, faceless 'people' are none other than your employees, managers and most definitely you. You see, a company may be able to work without a stable financing situation (for a short period of time). But it can never work if the individuals working in it are not dedicated to the task at hand.

After all, it's an undeniable fact that human errors are prone to happen when a person operates a toxic environment, is overburdened or under pressure. Thus, building a healthy and happy work environment should be your main objective when you intend to boost your productivity.

3. The Consumers

Next, your customers are a big part of this dynamic. You probably think that this is because a large pool of customers leads to more sales which in turn, get you more revenue. This is just a small section of the kind of influence they have on the bottom line.

The feature that we want you to focus on is productivity. Now, in this situation it is all about the invaluable feedback that the consumers provide. Your job is to listen to their complaints and address their problems. How does this benefit the business?

Well, for starters, the customers are the best source to learn about the problems in the product. Apart from that, they might direct your attention to the problem zones in your business.

Subsequently, your task becomes easier once you get an idea of what is going wrong in the customer's journey. Taking care of these pestering problems will ensure that the next customer comes out satisfied.

Plus, keeping an eye out for these things ensures that you overcome productivity issues as soon as they emerge.

4. The Production

In the end, your production capability is primarily responsible for the bottom line. That's because unlike abstract factors like customer satisfaction and employee attitude, the products and services are tangible goods.

That's why you must keep a strict check on the number of products that get manufactured within a certain time span. And the time it takes to get them to the customers. Thus, you can say that it isn't *just* about the production; it is all the other things that get tied with it.

For instance,

- How soon do goods get delivered?
- Is the packaging secure?

- How fast do the products sell?
- Are your men responsible for installation?
- How well does your pricing suit your services?

In a nutshell, productivity in association with your products and services is all about the promptness and feasibility. In other words, you can't expect to be productive if your money and time result in low-quality products even if they are greater in quantity. That's because this will have a direct impact on your sales.

The Bottom Line

To sum it up, productivity is an essential element that boots your sales. Basically, it helps you to recover the initial cost at a faster rate because the whole team is engaged in performing well. In addition to that, you'll be producing high-quality work that ensures customer satisfaction. Therefore, it's safe to assume that productivity will be giving you an edge over the competition. That's because you'll be doing things at a faster, better, and professional rate.

Now, that you know how important productivity is you should start integrating it into your business plan. The key to making this happen is by ensuring that you set goals that are achievable and practical. This kind of notion requires a whole lot of planning and a dedicated team that knows how to make each minute count. However, this can only be done if you have the right focus and a group of advisors who have the foresight to devise a plan for long-term results.

The next chapter is all about setting a game plan that delivers.

Chapter 2: The Game Plan: How to Be Productive from the Get Go?

Most people consider life as a competition. They wish to do things better and achieve their goals faster than their peers. Think of it as an ego boost that proves to the world that they are more successful than the others. The business industry has a similar opinion in regards to their relationship with competitors. They wish to outrun their rivals by drawing in more customers and completing more targets than the others in the market.

In other words, running a business isn't any different from sports. That's why just like sportsmen, you should work according to a strategy in order to win big. This strategy is dubbed as the 'game plan' which sets all your actions into motion. Moreover, it helps you to gain a footing in the market before you start taking any risks.

1. What Should You Visualize to Secure a Stable Bottom Line?

A short answer to this would be devising a game plan. You need to sit down and sketch out a strategy that overlooks your annual (or five-year) goals. This advance planning gives you a rough idea of what to expect and do in the coming year(s).

Business experts believe that it's the best way to figure out how to maintain a stable financial stand in the market. That's because it gives you a holistic view of the company's performance. You'll have a better understanding who does what and which areas require immediate attention. Basically, you'll be designing a scheme that incorporates different business elements that need to come together to produce consistent work in a designated time frame.

Like the business plan, your game plan is all about the company goals, strategies and the time duration estimated to accomplish the goals. But instead of a formal legal paper, this outline is roughly sketched at the back of your minds or on a whiteboard during the business meetings. That's because many businessmen label it as an informal plan of action that doesn't have legal bindings. As it's more about how the company wishes to operate rather than being a legal binding for the whole team.

This kind of flexibility is prudent for business managers as it allows them to have room for improvement. So that they may fix, adjust and modify the game plan according to the circumstances that arise during the operation. This kind of rough setup is a countermeasure that prevents major setbacks in case the company fails to meet the set goals. In other words, your business is prepared to accommodate anything and everything required to boost performance and production.

2. What's on Your Game Plan?

Here is everything that your game plan should cover:

1. The Purpose:

One of the main reasons why businesses fail to deliver is because they lose focus in the middle of their journey to create something substantial for their customers. This is a fairly common occurrence that happens when companies don't have their priorities straightened out. This could be because they work primarily for monetary gains and success.

A mindset like this is bound to undermine the power of customer satisfaction. Thus, you end up with an unsatisfactory turnout that isn't accepted by the consumer base. So you'll be losing money and consumers when you start work without having a clear objective in mind.

Therefore, it's better to start every project with a sense of purpose.

Try to find answers to questions like these:

- Who is your target?
- How can you solve their problems?
- What will you achieve?
- What services do you offer?

These answers will be your go-to source of motivation. They will help you remember why you are working on a certain project in the first place and also how you aspire to garner customer interest with the end results.

2. The Goals:

Aren't goals and purpose the same thing? The two terms might be interchangeable during conversations; they symbolize completely different things in the business world. That's because your purpose and mission is the philosophy that drives you to work. Many consider it an abstract notion that holds value in the company's brand story or culture.

On the other end, your goals are the tangible gains and profits you aim for. This could be anything from the number of products you wish to sell to the number of new customers you wish to convert. However, keep in mind that your goals are not wishful thinking. They have to be practical and achievable in the real world. Otherwise, you will be setting yourself up for disappointment. And that doesn't just lose your company's morale but it hinders productivity too.

That's because your employees will start questioning the purpose of their efforts if the goals appear to be impossible to accomplish.

3. Tools:

Tools are all the things that help your company to function properly. This includes everything from raw materials, labor to the strategies you are going to implement. They are basically the assets that support your company's work and development. You need to know what they are and how to utilize them in order to enhance productivity.

Why is this part of the game plan? A wise businessman always tracks and monitors the amount of money that he invests in his business. We'll be coming to that later but one way to evaluate the required funds is by estimating how much you'll need. And the only way to do that is by having a rough idea of all that needs to be added in the itinerary.

Moreover, you might even want to list trends, new upgrades, and advance equipment in this section. It will help you keep track of the new installations that the company may need in the near future. Additionally, maybe the new installations will actually pave the way for cost-effective solutions for the company.

4. Budget:

The budget is evidently the big bad wolf of all business plans. It can eat up all your prospective plans in an instant if you let it get out of hand. At least that is what most people tell us when they face a financial crisis due to mismanagement. That is why we suggest that you create a feasible budget before you launch your projects. After all, no company can survive without a substantial budget that finances all its needs.

A good budget covers every nitty gritty corner of the business expenditures. It is crucial that your budgeting is cost-effective and puts thought into each penny spent. Or else you will come out with a highly unattractive net income.

5. Deadline:

Productivity is entirely based on the time it takes to get things done. So naturally, your elusive deadlines are significantly important for the game plan. In fact, they kind of lay the foundation for the amount of time and money you will be spending to complete an assignment. This is why urgent based orders are given preference over deadlines that are a month away.

With that being said, deadlines are not just about time and money. They are also responsible for creating a schedule for you and your team. It allows you to devise a set routine that supports efficiency. It is safe to assume that without a timeframe your work pace might not be as productive as you want it to be. Moreover, the lack of deadlines often reduces the motivation and results in procrastination. That is because workers simply don't care when the work isn't required for submission at the end of the day.

Plus, deadlines help managers to monitor the work performance of each employee.

To sum it up, a well-designed game plan tries to accommodate almost all the variables that influence your company's productivity. Once these things become clear it will be easy for you to produce results and deliver them to the customers. However, there is no hard and fast rule regarding the points listed in your game plan. You are not obliged to implement all of them neither should you force the team to meet the target if you are lagging behind. Not only with that upset the workforce but it will also have a negative impact on the quality of the work they produce.

3. The Money Matters You Must Consider

Like we mentioned earlier, budgeting can create a big obstacle in your business ventures. Without a substantial budget, you can't set about to do the things you wish to do. That is why it's essential that you keep an eye on your bank account whenever you conduct a business transaction.

***These are some of the effective ways to prevent budget issues:**ns*

1. Setting Boundaries

Business owners are stereotypically considered to be very rich. That's because their business transactions all begin with a four to six digit figure. But that doesn't necessarily mean that they will always stay that way. This is why it is highly important to set a strict budget plan that helps you sustain your 'rich' status.

One tip for entrepreneurs is to always make a budget plan before they launch their business. Your plan must include these things all expenses related to operations, marketing campaigns, types of equipments, investments, and other subsidiary payments you are accountable for.

The budget provides you with a figure that will dominate most of your business deals. You'll know how much you have and how much you can afford to spend on a particular venture. Moreover, it allows you with a rough estimate to the company's net earnings at the end of the year. So that you can get a clearer image of how well you performed.

What if you don't stick to a budget? Our experience has taught us that a boundary-less budget is highly deceptive. It fools business owners into thinking that they have a lot more in the bank. When in reality they are much closer to hit rock bottom.

Therefore, it is better to conform to a budget. The most successful businesses are those that oblige by this rule. They free themselves of the headache of turning their finances into a chaotic mess that they can't possibly clear with loans.

2. The Overhead Expenses

Business experts believe that reducing overhead expenses has a positive impact on the company's bottom line. Overhead expenses are every penny that goes into dealing with the daily requirements of your business. This includes everything from high priced insurance policies, annual leases to the price of a small repair. It goes without saying that your maintenance bills and utility bills are all part of this financial category.

Can overhead expenses blow your budget? They sure can!

You see, it doesn't matter if you are running a successful business or not. The annual overhead expense is a mandatory fixture in your budget. While the monthly ones like utility bills and repairs may fluctuate according to the needs of that particular period. On the whole, you are required to pay a hefty price each year on things that aren't exclusively linked to the production of your products. This means that you can try to keep a low profile during overhead purchases.

Not only will it save a lot of money but it will indirectly reduce your stress over pending payments. So in a way, you'll get more time to cater to the other areas of your business.

Now, the question is 'how do you cut down overhead expenses?' The answer is pretty simple; you eliminate the things you don't necessarily need to be productive. You'd be surprised to see how decluttering your office space can actually reduce this sort of expenditure.

Here are a couple of financially prudent modifications you can make in your office:

- **Reduce Rent:** Small businesses can cut down rent costs by sharing a joint office space with other start-ups. You can also opt for low-cost commercial areas that have affordable rent.
- **Conserve Energy:** Improve your utility bills by using eco-friendly methods in your everyday life. This includes using solar panels for electricity, conserving energy and recycling your waste.
- **Eliminate Extravagance:** Many businesses incorporate a luxurious flair to their office space. This means you are privy to installing random flimsy fixtures just for appearance sake. These things need constant attention and repairs to stay put. The best way to reduce this cost is by opting for furniture, architecture and technology that is functional rather than recreational.

Here are a handful of other financial tips that help manage your business better:

- Always save money for rainy days and emergencies to ensure the company doesn't drown in debts

- Ensuring that the product pricing remains competitive without seeming too expensive
- Making sure that the employees and their benefits aren't compromised during budget cuts
- Promptly paying your taxes and other obligatory payments to prevent embarrassment

In short, the art of managing a healthy business plan lies in its stable financial diet. You don't want to overdo or under do the budget plans by making irreversible errors.

The Bottom Line

On the whole, your game plan is all about the initial prep and plans you make for your business. You can think of it as a blueprint for the coming year or a set of goals for the near future.

On the contrary, many companies try to create a game plan that makes predictions for the distant future. The interval between the 'now and then' scenarios is roughly around five to ten years. We think that this is a good practice that prepares you for the long haul. But doing so should not blind you for the things you need to take into consideration in the imminent one. This is especially true, for budget plans and time-sensitive aspects of your business.

Once you have figured all these things out, you should do your best to practically act upon the plan. Your responsibility is to ensure that managers supervise, workers work and the production crew produces things like clockwork.

However, simply planning what you want from your business ventures do not guarantee a substantial net income. You have got to put some effort into maintaining the momentum. The remaining chapters illustrate some effective strategies and solutions to meet these requirements.

So let's get to work!

Chapter 3: The Management: Are Your Managers Doing Their Job?

Are your managers doing their job?

Okay, we agree that this might be a tough question for many companies that consider managers as the top-dogs. They are an elite class of workers who are untouchable in the company hierarchy. That means they are rarely questioned by authorities when something goes wrong.

When in reality, management is a crucial player in your company's productivity rate. You can't expect the company to make sales and perform well if you have got irresponsible managers leading the pack. Similarly, many a time it is the manager's and not the worker's fault.

Thus, instead of playing the blame game through your skewed deduction skills, you should be crafting your manager's rapport with the rest of the team. Believe us, a well-balanced company dynamics is the key to better productivity.

In our books, it is practically impossible to run a productive business without the help of your managers. That is why we dedicate this chapter to understanding the *hows* and *whys* of productive management. First, we'll inform you about the tell-tale signs that indicate mismanagement. Then we'll highlight the new managing practices and techniques that have a positive impact on the company's work rate. At the end of it all, we hope that you'll learn a thing or two about developing a managing team that knows how to inspire the workers.

1. What Role Does Management Play Here?

Managers are as the designation suggests, the 'leaders' of the company. The whole team has to follow their commands and oblige to the tasks they assign. So it is easy to assume that changing their behavior will have a direct impact on the rest of the team. Plus, it is a much more tangible way to approach productivity issues when it comes to one's work performance.

With that being said, the definition of management has certainly shifted in the past few decades. Managers are no longer restricted to 'supervise and delegate' work. Nor are they the oldest and most experienced employees of the company. In the modern era of the corporate world, managers are leaders with vision and intuition. That's why sometimes age become inconsequential.

Now, this might not sit well with the senior members of the working staff but that is what it is in the new millennia. Therefore, it is highly advisable that your managers learn how to deal with the employees in a genuine and authentic manner.

Authenticity is a way that allows them to handle situations with authority and camaraderie. This ensures that the people under them don't feel like the management is imposing rules and regulations on them. This sort of mutual appreciation club helps boosts the team's morale as they feel recognized and valued. We'll delve deeper into this aspect of the company culture a bit later in the book.

Now, let's focus just on management.

Think of managers as coaches. A good coach sticks with the team through and through. They are out on the field playing and practicing new strategies. They evaluate the different members of the team and have a good grasp of how well an individual performs. Not to forget that they are always ready to push the players further by boosting their morale.

Moreover, they have a knack of looking at the team in a holistic manner and they know that each player brings something valuable to the table.

In a similar manner, your company needs managers who are willing to emulate the same persona. They need to lead the team in a way that shows they know and appreciate their employees. More importantly, they must acknowledge all the little efforts employees put in to hit the targets.

2. A Manager's Dos and Don'ts

Here are a handful of managing tactics that effectively boost productivity:

1. Steer Clear from Micromanaging

Did you know? Most employees confess that they get nervous around managers. This anxiety often leads them to make blunders that could have been avoided in the first place.

This revelation is vital in understanding the psychology of most employees. Usually, the new ones tend to get flustered during interactions with their seniors. That is why it is important to give your employees some space during work hours. Does that means closing doors and backing off?

Nope. The clear cut solution is to facilitate partial autonomy in the workroom. This means that although managers are in charge of the project, they should not hover. Instead, try to set timely meetings to see how the work is progressing and then let the workers work. It is a pretty simple strategy that encourages productivity. The reason being that without the manager's constant meddling, the employees are able to take ownership over their work. Not only does that help them gain confidence but it encourages them to take responsibility for what they do.

So instead of working as dictators, your managers get to supervise a team that thinks for on their own. This in turn stimulates innovative ideas and creative thoughts in the workers. And all these roads lead to optimized performance.

2. Keep the Door Open

Nobody likes a manager who comes late to work and then stays cooped up in their room.

Doesn't that negate the purpose of the first rule? Not really!

Good managers know the difference between micromanaging and effective managing. That is why instead of standing over the team's shoulders, they beckon them to come and have a chat. This allows them to handle internal affairs without creating a public scene. For we all know how suppressing problems and angry employees can cause a whole lot of drama in the long run.

An easy way to calm disgruntled employees is to help them find a medium to vent their issues. Not only does it have a cathartic effect on them. But your managing staff will be able to fix the situation before it blows up.

Does this really work? It does!

You'll be surprised to see how open employees can be if you give them a chance to share their opinions with the managers. This could be anything from asking for solutions regarding a taxing project or offering constructive criticism towards some managing mistakes. Such discussions give the manager a better insight to what the team thinks and what obstacles they face on a daily basis. These are things you won't be able to learn if you sit inside the office without a care in the world about the employees.

The key here is to set your ego aside and listen to what your team has to say. At the end of the day, it is up to you to create a healthy and productive environment.

3. Evaluate, Asses and Comment

Did you know? One of the biggest setbacks a company can face is when they start losing out on good employees. Many a time, the brilliant newcomers you recruited start to burn out in the middle of the year. This kind of problem usually arises when managers don't make efforts to evaluate and asses their works.

The dead silence from the higher-ups causes the work progress to become stagnant over time. That is because each employee needs some form of affirmation or encouragement to let them know that they are on the right track. This allows them to feel valued in the company.

Moreover, assessing work performances helps managers delegate the tasks in a better manner. Their evaluations point out the top performers and help them narrow down the weak links. This kind of information works wonders when utilized in the right way.

As you get a chance to pair off teams and appoint leaders that will get the job done right the first time around.

In addition to that, monthly or bi-annual assessments help the management to make unbiased judgment calls during appraisals and budget cuts.

4. Set Tangible Goals

Did you know? Setting high goals almost always lead to better performance.

The only problem is that many managers start putting impossible targets for the team. As a result, this kind of grand proposal causes the team to feel disheartened. Since in their minds, the manager is setting them up for a defeat. Therefore, it is important to know how the team will react when you wind them up for an ambitious project.

How to create a successful game plan for the team?

- ***Start small:*** You might be confident in your team but setting them an over-the-top target can be a recipe for disaster. That is why it is best to follow the age-old strategy of 'slow and steady wins the race' and then increase the stakes as the team grows.

- *Place milestones:* Sometimes year-long projects start to drag and the employees start to lose interest. That's why it is better to create smaller milestones to help track their progress. This lets them celebrate little victories and boosts their morale.
- *Lead the way:* Try to act upon what you preach in the boardrooms. You must be working as hard as them if you want them to cross the finish line.
- *Share Point of Views:* You must discuss the team's views about the targets you give them. Try to negotiate a figure that is unanimously agreed upon.
- *Deadlines:* Goals should always be time-sensitive. This adds an element of urgency and a sense of accountability in the workers.

On the whole, learn to aim for targets that are challenging yet attainable. This helps your employees to grow as individuals and develop their skill set in a positive way.

5. Discussions Come Before Repercussions

The last thing you should remember is the fact that discussions are one of the best ways to optimize productivity. We aren't talking about board meetings where you dictate the employees on what they have to do and what you'll be changing in the coming months. No, that is probably one of the worst ways to manage a team of intellects and professionals.

The key to getting everyone on the same page is by conducting proper discussion sessions. The kind that let employees speak on behalf of the team and let their doubts out about a recent change. Isn't this the same thing as point number two? Not really, in this scenario, you'll be making decisions as a group.

Business insiders believe that collective decisions over conflicting issues are a great way to boost workplace productivity. As they allow you to build a healthy work culture that expedites their performance instead of hindering them.

How? Well, think about it. Happy employees always lead to a healthier workplace environment. As you won't be facing disgruntled employees trying to bring you down or quit jobs when something doesn't sit well with them.

In a nutshell, a good manager is always open to discussions, negotiations and facilitating employee needs. One way to adopt this kind of demeanor is by abiding the rules of authentic leadership.

2. Why Is Authentic Leadership the Answer?

You might have heard this buzzword being dropped at some leadership conference. Or maybe you read an article that cited the significance of authentic leadership in the present world. Odds are you still don't understand what exactly this term entails and why should you be investing in these new-age authentic leaders. So let's enlighten you with this wonderful new discovery that is getting hyped up in the past few decades.

We'll start off with the basic definition of this leadership strategy. As the name suggests, this is a leadership approach that encourages leaders to embrace their authenticity. So you don't really have to hire new managers to get an authentic leadership front. Rather you must train your current leaders and managers to adopt genuine tactics when they work with their employees.

So who is an authentic leader? It is someone who builds their authority on the foundation of honest conduct, sincere relationships and ethical values. These people that prefer to come to work donning their real-life personality. They don't shy away from appearing enthusiastic or honest about how they feel about the work you do. They feel that creating a good rapport with their team is better than opting for a dictatorship regime that only demeans the team.

As a result, people start to get drawn by their authentic conduct. So they become the inspiring influence that pulls the team towards a positive direction.

How do they accomplish this feat? Why are they an asset in your company's hierarchy? These are probably a few of the questions that may have come to your mind when we explained what authentic leadership means. That is because is in this day and age, people are rarely authentic when it comes to running the business world. So appointing an authentic leader sounds like a catch-22 as they couldn't possibly survive in a cut-throat environment of the business world. Could they?

You'd be surprised to hear that they absolutely can make a difference and ensure that the results lay in your favor.

That's because these authentic leaders have:

1. Clearer Vision

Authentic leaders craft clear-cut visions that aren't wrapped in any cheap tactics or ulterior motives. Rather than glossing their visions with superficial aims they lead the team with an easy and attainable idea. These visions address the approaching future in a much more logical way.

This focused vision helps the team attain its goals with the utmost ease. Additionally, the team invests more in a manager that leads them with the sheer force of his words and plans.

2. Higher Engagement

Normally, managers only interact with the workers when they are needed. Not only does it hinder the two-way conversation but it also instills a sort of hierarchy in the line of work. This only gives space to a toxic work-relationship to build over time.

On the other hand, the authentic leaders wish to be a part of the team from the get-go. Their friendlier and much more open approach in their field is appreciated by the rest of the crew. In addition to that, they pay close attention to building relationships and interacting with each and every member of the team.

Consequently, higher engagement helps shape and polish innovative ideas in the office. This directly influences the productivity and performance rate of the company.

3. Honest Opinions

In this diplomatic age, authentic leaders are like a breath of fresh air. Their honest conduct and truthful revelations boost the credibility of your company. So not only will they be appreciated by the workers. But this trait will also be acknowledged by your business associates. That is because authentic leaders have a way of standing out from the pack. They are there to put in hard work and express honest opinions no matter what the other people say. It is this kind of work ethic and sincerity that helps them emerge amidst the cookie-cutter crowd.

As a result, more people would wish to connect with your company as it is lead by people who really care about the job. This, in turn, will have a positive impact on the company's productivity.

The Bottom Line

On the whole, you'd be surprised to see how a tiny effort on the management's part can help boost your team's morale. The reason is strictly tied up with the old belief that you should 'serve others and others will serve you.' That's why it is important that you pay heed to the kind of feedback your workers give about their managers.

Doing so will help you detect the problem areas of your company. This then can be addressed in a holistic way that aims to cultivate a team spirit. Moreover, you will learn to train employees to work collectively as a single unite of like-minded people. Subsequently, these efforts will work in line to improve bottom-line productivity.

With all of this being said, your work doesn't end here. That's because the company operates on a two-way street (three-way if we count the customers). So you should be keeping an eye on the workers and promoting a work environment that helps workers thrive on a day to day basis.

How do you do that? We'll explain the secrets to unlock your workers' potential in the next chapter.

Chapter 4: The Workforce: Is Your Work Environment Build for Productivity?

"Don't pick a job with great vacation time.

Pick one that doesn't need escaping."

This is one of those 'dream job' quotes that often wind up on your social media feed. You know the ones that encourage people to pick passion over their profession. It inspires them to choose jobs where their satisfaction is the company's first priority. The chances are that your employees are looking at similar quotes at this very moment. Plus, they are probably comparing their work life with this quote.

This kind of evaluation has the power to make or break your bottom-line productivity.

Do you want to know how? Well, for starters, employees calling in sick or ditching work early are apparent red flags for your business. You can very well believe that the habitual absence of a particular employee is a sign that they are unhappy with the work situation. This lack of presence, physical or otherwise, directly affects their performance. As they are less likely to commit to their work if they are more prone to fleeing the scene at a moment's notice.

So how should you tackle this problem? Should you fire them on the spot? Or you might call them in and give them a warning? Do you humiliate them in front of the team?

Honestly speaking, none of these actions will actually work on these disengaged employees. These tactics might even agitate them further. Now, we know that some of you may think that a confrontation is sufficient enough to reform a stray employee. But the fact of the matter is that they are bound to go back to their old ways within a week after your meeting.

You might have already experienced this kind of situation in your office before.

We believe that the best way to handle this sensitive situation is by finding the root of the problem. More often than not, you will learn that your work culture and the environment is the main culprit in this unsteady equation. That is why we suggest that it is high time that you do start investing in your corporate culture.

Try to build a work environment and culture that nurtures the employees rather than suffocates them. You need to provide them with some space, a breath of fresh air and lots of healthy relationships. Factors like these may seem insignificant to you since you believe that offices are a place of work, not socialization. Yet, these little details are essential in creating a healthy environment for the team.

You may still be of the opinion that 'why should you bother about the comfort of your employees?'

After all, you can always recruit a new employee. That is what many old-school businessmen think when we suggest a change in the company. In order to provide an answer to them, we always bring up the statistics that show how well culture-conscious companies perform in comparison to those not attuned to their employees' grievances. Additionally, it has been observed that a better culture cultivates a better work ethic. This eventually leads to these companies outperforming their rivals in any industry.

What's more? Even world-renowned tech-firms like Google and Apple are all about building a cultured environment that keeps their workers happy. With inspirations like these, we think you would be motivated to give this suggestion a chance.

Wouldn't you?

Still not convinced?

Let us help you make this decision by pointing out key variables that impact your team's productivity.

1. How Does Corporate Culture Affect Productivity?

In order to understand the link between corporate culture and productivity, you need to first understand what the term implies.

In a holistic way, the company culture is strongly linked to abstract and tangible elements of your work environment. It includes things like the values, beliefs, behavior and attitudes of a company that has a drastic impact on your bottom-line productivity.

But also consists of the various other elements like employee benefits, the surroundings, and various facilities provided to the employees. On the whole, it is anything and everything that affects the way your employees perceive the company.

Here are a handful of ways in which corporate culture impedes work performance:

1. Absenteeism

Does your company keep track of your employees' attendance? If they don't then they certainly should because absenteeism might as well be the plague that eats up company profits.

It is no hidden secret that most employees are prone to calling in 'sick' when they need a break from their mundane work environment. This often happens when the company has wrapped up a major project. As that is a time when employees feel burned out and wish to stay home rather than starting another tedious task. Other than that, employees may seek a change from their stressful environment.

What if your employees are really sick? Well then, in cases of some chronic illness, we advise you to allow them flexible hours. This kind of effort on your part encourages them to come back to work soon after they start to recover.

Moreover, try to devise a well-planned attendance policy that promotes productivity. Some companies offer their workers a bonus salary when they are called to work during the weekend/holidays. Others might even provide free meals during overtime.

So basically, your aim here is to eliminate the problem areas that might be increasing absenteeism. You should also ensure that the employees know that creating stable work-home balance will be profitable for them. However, instead of forcing them to come to work, you need to create a safe environment that they don't wish to change.

2. Job Stress

Whether it is due to a high-end assignment or a horrid boss, stress is one of the main factors that decrease work productivity. You can easily vouch for the fact that many employees have left your company because they found the work 'too stressful'. Or that the kind of demands the employer expected was not something they signed up for. These and many other reasons are an indication that your company might be overworking its employees.

Have you heard all of this before? Of course, you have! But the question is how exactly you dealt with these situations. In most cases, employers ignore the signs and have carried on overburdening other employees. At the end of which, they are left with no more than a handful of workers that stay with the company for more than a year. That sounds rough, doesn't it? Not only does it hinder your growth as a company but it means that you will be spending most of your time training new employees. This kind of setback blows your chances of harvesting a stable bottom-line productivity in the long run.

That's why it is important to diffuse stressful situations by:

- Discussing the workload with your employees and offering flexible hours
- Resolving office politics before they escalate into cold wars
- Enlisting rules that help eliminate the stress factors (e.g. noisy employees, stuffy environment, etc.)

The main idea is that you take well-thought countermeasures as soon as you notice that an employee is slipping from their usual work rate.

3. Physical Environment

Your office spaces are a prominent part of the corporate culture. Therefore, they unintentionally become the reason why many of your employees feel so disengaged with their work. The contributing factors lay in the seating arrangement, temperature, noise, and also the food scene of a particular company.

Wait, how is this possible? It isn't as absurd as it sounds, really. If you think about it, your workers spend a good part of their day in your office buildings. Most of the time is spent sitting in their cubicles, working away like a hamster in a wheel. Not only does this day to day activity become boring and bland after some time. But the drab looking walls and harsh lighting might drain their energies when they stay inside for long hours.

It is for this very reason why the new-age organizations are gradually directing their attention towards creative and interactive spaces for their employees. They plan to build a kind of office that harmonizes work and recreation in the same building.

Most of the blueprints aim to:

- ***Add Fun Elements:*** Building a recreational center for employees to sit in their downtime. This could be an indoor game room or a TV-lounge with an entertainment center.
- ***Satisfying Hunger Pangs:*** Putting up vending machines to satisfy their mid-work cravings. You should also have coffee/tea stations to

give them their daily dose of caffeine.

- ***Fitness Quotient:*** Have a small gym attached to the workspace. This helps your workers to blow off some steam when they are all wound up with work.
- ***A Touch of Color: Incorporating*** wall art and encouraging employees to decorate their cubicles offers an aesthetic comfort in a way that plain old white walls never can.
- ***Nature's Nurture:*** Add potted plants, use natural lighting and keep windows open to stop the office from feeling too stuffy.

On the whole, you want to ensure that your employees stay comfortable and happy when they work relentlessly to meet their targets. Otherwise, you know what they say, 'all work and no play makes' employees duller each day. This then leads to a low productivity rate and high absenteeism.

4. Employee's Health

Are all your employees on a collective life insurance plan? Does the company provide them with substantial health insurance?

The fact that your worker's health is your biggest asset is not exactly a far-fetched idea. Since their health is directly linked with the way they do their jobs. A small survey of your employee's attendance sheet will tell you that healthy employees tend to be happier than unhealthy ones. Thus, it will do you good to create health plans and enroll them in wellness programs that ensure that their health stays on track.

These are a few things you can do to help boost their health:

- Provide them with a feasible health insurance plan
- Give them a fair amount of sick leaves and paid vacations
- Try to instill healthy eating habits by appointing a health-conscious chef (if daily meals are part of the corporate benefit)
- Offer maternity and paternity leaves to employees
- Calling in counselors and guest lecturers to help instill healthy habits in the company culture

In their entirety, these health benefits are good indicators of how much value a company gives to its employees. You might think that they are a bit much when you consider the expenses. But choosing feasible health plans and taking reasonable steps towards a healthy initiative shall do the trick. That is because your goal is to provide the employees with a safety net. It assures them that they are well taken care of. Or else, they will be moving on to other companies that have a better understanding of what they need.

Once you have ticked off all these things, you will start noticing a positive change in the overall behavior of your employees. Like the fact that they will be stepping into the premises with a happier mood and will be much more receptive to your inputs.

Now, that we have worked all these things out, it is time to look at the actual players in this game. These are none other than the employees whose work performance is closely tied up to your bottom-line productivity.

That is why the next question is:

2. How Do You Judge Your Team's Contributions?

You might have smoothened wrinkles and cleared out obstructions that were hindering your company's work performance in regards to the company culture. But what if you are still underwhelmed by the efforts they put in each day?

This is the perfect time to set up a meeting and discuss their work performance. However, before you start calling them in, you must know if your evaluations are accurate enough to demand a change. More importantly, have you been recording statistics and calculating their career graph on the side.

If the answer is no, then you must learn how to evaluate the employee performance before you shower them with criticism. That is because your employees won't necessarily bite their tongue when you accuse them of irresponsible work ethic or mishandling of projects. In such cases, they would actually prefer to see the evidence that proves your claims. Besides this, this kind of record is beneficial for both the management and the staff. It helps them to track, maintain and improve their work over time. That's why it is important for you to formulate an effective assessment strategy. One way to do this is by setting certain criteria for the evaluation procedure. In this way, the people conducting the assessments will know what they have to do. Plus, this procedure assures your workers that the matter is being dealt with objectivity.

Here are four steps that need to be taken for an effective evaluation:

1. Create Evaluation Forms

The first step of any evaluation process is composing a proper evaluation format. You need to create some sort of standard form that managers can fill in to assess their employees. This method ensures that the assessments are conducted impartially at all times. In addition to that, we suggest that you focus on the factors that are directly linked to their performance. Bringing up other issues would only lead to digressions.

But how do you decide what goes in the form? A good practice is to compose evaluation forms. For instance, a salesman is going to be judged by how many sales he makes within a month and the number of new customers he recruited. On the other hand, the employee with a desk job will be judged according to the projects he closed. Even though the job set is different, you'll have to create a general form that matches every employee.

Therefore, you're most likely to discuss the skillset, quality, and quantity of the work each employee does. But there is no harm in commenting on their work habits too e.g. attitude, behavior during work hours and punctuality. Highlight the ones that might influence their performance whether it is negatively or positively. However, the appraiser must give valid reasons for their assessments. As stated earlier, employees appreciate feedback that is backed by evidence.

2. Performance Measurements

This is the next step of your form. Instead of giving your managers an empty space to fill up the areas, you should create a metric system for evaluations. Not only does it reduce the time taken to fill the form but it also provides accurate evaluations. You can opt for a numerical system that marks your employee's performance in each division like in percentage. Or you might use certain descriptors to measure their work (like excellent, good, average, and poor).

Of course, this system only works if you have chosen components that can be measured. In areas like work habits, you may choose a lax approach. That means the managers are permitted to comment on these abstract areas without a marking scheme.

Furthermore, there are few things to keep in mind during this process. The evaluation forms must be able to collect both quantitative and qualitative data. This ensures that the appraisal has happened in a holistic way. Secondly, always keep a previous record of the employee's performance at hand. This helps you to have a better idea of how much progress they have made during their employment.

Lastly, ensure that the assessment scale and your expectations for each employee are realistic. You can't expect them to pay attention to the appraisals if the standards are set too high.

How do you measure the employee performance? It should be done within a controlled environment and with a more customized rather than a configured system of appraisals.

3. Establish Guidelines for Feedback

Once the forms are composed, you'll be distributing it to the related authorities. In most cases, the appraisals are made by managers and team leaders. Be sure to set a proper committee of reviewers (2 to 4 members) who overlooks the evaluations. This group should include the head of the company, someone from the supervisory staff and the respective managers. To be on the safe side, it is recommended that you set some rules of conduct. This ensures that the feedback is accurate and untampered due to biases.

After that, each appraisal meeting must follow a pattern. Not only is this a more professional approach but the routine ensures that you cover all aspects of the evaluation form. Moreover, it gives you a chance to conduct the meetings in a proper manner.

Here is a routine that works like clockwork:

1. Provide the employee with a summary of their performance on the basis of the evaluation form.

2. Initiate the meeting by highlighting positive areas of their work and appreciate them. Then broach the areas where there is room for improvement. In both cases, support your remarks with solid pieces of evidence.

3. Set the momentum for the next meeting by giving them targets. This can be done by creating a rough sketch of how their performance chart must look like in the next meeting.

4. Try to give them an opportunity to bring their own concerns to the table. Their feedback will let you know how you can support their performance.

In the end, the trick of getting through these meetings is by acting calmly. You need to prepare yourself for situations where the employees might not accept your criticism. They'll either react in a stubborn manner and deny everything or accuse you of some misconduct. Some may even be overwhelmed by the assessments or go into a panic mode when you start talking about new targets. In any case, your aim is to stay calm and encourage them for the coming months.

4. Creating a Schedule

Is there an ideal time to conduct your evaluation meetings?

Not really. Your schedules can be arranged throughout the year. Most companies prefer to hold these meetings at the end of the year. This helps them assess how well their employees performed in a particular year and then motivate them for the next one. Others call up their employees during their work anniversaries. So the event doubles up as an assessment and as a cause for celebration. The second option works well for most employers. That's because it allows them to spread out the evaluation work throughout the year.

Other than that, you may also decrease the time lapse your meetings. Instead of arranging annual meetings you could conduct them twice a year. This strategy lets you evaluate their progress in a better way. Plus, monitoring them within brief intervals will mean that you'll have a tighter grasp at how well they perform. So if a few of them start slipping at the middle of the year, it doesn't take you a year to address the issue.

In the end, make sure that all the employees get evaluated on the set dates. You can't skip/delay appraisals during the evaluation month. Doing so will probably create some tension or weaken their morale because it will look like they have been slighted by the management.

The Aftermath: Will Your Employees Take the Evaluations Seriously?

What if this strategy doesn't work? What if there is no change in their productivity?

A stagnant growth means that you need to emphasize on the importance of these discussions. This is especially true for those employees who aren't paying heed to your criticism. Once again, your strategy should be to enforce the significance of these meetings to the whole group. This will show them that the rules are the same for all of them

Now, it's quite normal to anticipate mixed reactions from the team about their respective evaluations. But at the end of the day, they must know that you expect the discussion to lead to positive outcomes. A good way to do this is by attaching a 'reward and punishment' method based on their performance.

What's the reward? Money is the biggest motivator in the workplaces. Therefore, you can add value to the meeting by linking them with increments/bonus salaries. This only works if your company has a policy that offers pay on merit instead of the years they have spent in the office. This direct link between money and merit provides them with a good incentive to work harder. Additionally, it will increase their enthusiasm for the evaluation. They might even start putting in more efforts in order to impress you and get the bonus.

What's the punishment? In all honesty, you can't expect the employees to be at their best behavior at all times. But you need to take strict action when their attitude has a negative effect on the company's productivity. On these instances, it is better to take strict action before things derail any further. Yet, firing them on the spot isn't a good option either. Start the disciplining them with simple warnings before signing them off with a termination letter.

The best route to go is by giving them a verbal warning and then a written one if the matter isn't resolved. These warnings should be given in private so they don't get embarrassed in front of their peers. After that, if they are still slacking off then a termination might be the only solution. However, this must always be the last resort. In each case, grant them three chances to rectify their mistakes and then let them go free.

Will this work? Yes, it will. This practice teaches your team that they will be held accountable for the kind of work they produce. Subsequently, they'll pay more attention to the feedback you give them after each meeting. So your strategy promotes their performance and instills a sense of ownership in the work they do.

On the whole, the evaluation strategy allows you to provide an unbiased and justifiable assessment of your employees. The main aim is to measure the contribution of your workforce and then develop a plan that improves it further. When done right, these performance evaluations can become a vital variable that boosts your bottom-line productivity. Moreover, it lets your employees know that you're watching and appreciating the work they do. Even the slightest bit of acknowledgment can go a long way in raising their morale.

3. How to Boost the Employee's Productivity? Okay, so you have already modified the work environment and also started assessing the team on a regular basis. Yet, despite all these efforts, there is still something lacking in the productivity department. What's going on? Who is to blame here? In each case, a different set of culprits may emerge.

Sometimes those projects might have got impeded due to an external factor. At other times it will be the consequence of poor planning. The list of reasons keeps changing according to the situation.

Nevertheless, here are three strategies that work wonders on your company's productivity levels.

1. The Training Sessions

Recruiting the top candidates doesn't guarantee stable bottom-line productivity. This is a myth that has been prevalent since ages. That's because they can't all be 'Jacks of all trades. This is why it is important that you arrange some training sessions for your team.

Firstly, have a standard training session on their orientation day. The main idea is to give them a heads up on what to expect on an average workday. You must also guide them throughout the first week on how work gets done in your company. In addition to that, new employees can have a go-to leader who can assist them during the probation period. These things ensure that the newcomers aren't left on their own in unfamiliar surroundings. Moreover, you'll put them at ease by making them understand that seeking help is not a weakness.

Next, have monthly training sessions with the whole staff/specific departments. You can teach them a new skillset or work on polishing the ones they already have. There are many other things you can work on via their training sessions. This includes remedial classes, introducing new software programs or ones that help boost teamwork. Apart from these, you can send some of them off for leadership conferences and industry-based workshops etc. This kind of exposure enhances their skills and boosts their confidence. Moreover, training is more effective when it's specifically linked to the skill the employee lacks.

In the end, you can't expect certain results without investing in the change yourself.

2. The Streamline Process

Is time management an issue in your office?

Of course, it is. It seems to be a global problem because most of us are tempted to procrastinate. Nonetheless, you can take some countermeasures to ensure that your team knows how to prioritize their work. The first thing to do is to simplify their workflow. Try to label the projects as 'urgent', 'important', 'last priority' etc so they know which tasks need more attention. You may also designate projects according to their capabilities. Or appoint team leaders that hold members check up on the progress during the day.

Basically, the 'streamline' process is any technique that pushes your employees to concentrate on their work. You can also use training sessions that help them tackle a busy workday or that deals with anxiety-attacks. The key here is to help them figure out how to keep their energy and productivity high at all times.

3. The Pat on the Back and Perks

Isn't an annual raise a perk? Yes, it is.

Yet, you can't deny the fact that on-the-job privileges have a direct effect on their work. These perks could be anything from office facilities, free lunches/outings to gift vouchers. You can have monthly competitions or weekly round-ups that put the best workers in the spotlight.

Why does this work? Well, nothing boosts productivity like a good old competitive spirit. People like to win things and one-up their peers. This holds true for situations that might not have a big reward. The thing is that people crave attention and acknowledgements. This technique gives them exactly that. They'd appreciate the acknowledgements and admiring glances from their colleagues. Moreover, if there is an actual prize attach to it then you know they might work even harder for this friendly match.

What's more? The great thing about these perks is that everyone has an equal chance to receive rewards. This creates enough incentive for all the employees to work harder during the month. And even if they don't win, you'll be providing them with role models. Then there is also the fact that they can work harder the next time around.

Basically, it is a win-win situation for everyone!

The Bottom Line

In a nutshell, you need to invest in your employees if you want the best results. These investments include tangible things like cultivating a performance linked productive work environment and designing a better office space. Other than that, you can enable their productivity by monitoring and evaluating their performance through the proper channels.

Primarily, your employees must feel that they are valued members of the team. When you give them the respect they deserve and provide them with opportunities to grow. Then they will automatically be motivated to elevate their efforts. As a result, your team will start working like a well-oiled machine that covers the right amount of miles in the fastest time.

Now, that we have covered your human resources it is time to direct your attention to other aspects of the company. Strengthening those factors can easily give you an edge over your competitors.

Do you want to know what they are? Then let's move on towards the next chapter.

Chapter 5: The Strategies: What Can You Do to Boost Productivity?

'Improved productivity means less human sweat, not more'

-Henry Ford

This is a pretty interesting quote that targets the flaw in our perception of productivity. You see, most businesses are under the impression that productivity is synonymous with manual labor. So they push their workforce to work longer hours and put in more efforts. To be honest, this kind of forceful productivity will only lead to sweating employees who are drained out of energy for the next day. The key to productivity as Mr. Ford suggests, is not overworking your employees. It actually lays in the efficiency of your team.

This means that they have to figure out a way to do generate results faster. We're looking at high-quality products manufactured in the shortest time. Not high quantity of products delivered in shabby presentations. Do you get where we are coming from?

Of course, you do! This kind of philosophy aligns with your dream of generating better products as quickly as you can. Now, up until this point in the book, we have been going over the various areas of productivity in the business sector. We have discussed the importance of having a vision and paid attention to your managers and employees.

Now, it is time to bring these key factors in parallel light. What we mean is that you have to adopt a business strategy that aligns your vision with the practical efforts the workers put in each day.

You see, the leader might have a vision in their head and will lead the pack accordingly. But no matter how foresighted you try to be, one can't predict the day to day challenges faced on the operational floors. Like having no electricity, running out of supplies, tax deductions and list of troubles can keep on going on for eternity.

Consequently, these daily hindrances have a negative impact on our promising game plan. Some even go as far as to say that it dampens any prospects of being productive. This all leads to unfinished projects and frequent delays. That in turn, reduces our bottom-line-productivity.

Who is at fault here? The answer doesn't necessarily point you in the right direction. That is because, in a company of thousands of employees, you rarely identify a single culprit. Plus, more often than not, your planning is at fault here. Upon further investigation, you will start noticing the misalignment between your business proposal and execution.

1. The Flaw in the Plan

Why did your plans fail?

There is a simple quote that is making waves on the internet, it goes something like this:

"Life is what happens when you are busy making other plans"

-John Lennon

This here is the answer to your question. Business owners and strategists are usually found getting excited over promising agendas. They are cooped up in their offices brainstorming brilliant new schemes that might provide them with better turnovers. The only problem is that while they are inside sketching out their plans, life has already gotten in the way of their proposed execution.

In most cases, this happens because you failed to understand the real-life circumstances that might come up. This could be anything from power breakdowns, political strikes, malfunctioning machines to the shortage of supplies. Even minuscule things like a missing paper clip could influence a chain of reactions that impede the company's productivity on the day to day basis.

Basically, a person sitting in the CEO seat will probably never objectively perceive the little roadblocks that come during the operations. This is why they tend to create game plans that are more whimsical than practical. It is partly because they want the team to achieve the impossible and mainly because they can't grasp how things actually play out during execution.

In other words, the whole operational phase is pretty complex. You can't expect things to run smoothly in the first go. That is why it is important for you to give your business plans and the team a little leeway. Give them space to modify execution when things go astray.

This is one way to overcome certain areas of misalignment. The other solution is to improve communications between all the players in your company. We are talking about transparent communication lines that clearly portray what happens at each phase.

You see, things will not work out if the higher-ups aren't aware of the mishaps happening in the factory. In a similar manner, the delivery team won't know what to do when there is a delay at your end. How can they pacify employees when they aren't sure if the product will be delivered? This is why it is essential that everyone makes an effort to communicate.

Each team needs to know what happens at each phase of the product's manufacturing process; tangible or intangible. This gives them a holistic view of the importance of the role they play. It also encourages them to take ownership of the work they do. Next, you must advise teams to promptly inform the other departments when there is a holdup. By keeping everyone in the loop, you will be ensuring that the final presentation is a team effort.

In addition to that, you will have an easier way to identify the problems when they do occur. Otherwise, you would be left wondering what went wrong and how it happened. Plus, it is more convenient to address and rectify discrepancies right after they occur then facing the consequences in the aftermath. Isn't it?

The key factors that retain the company's productivity are:

- Communication
- Flexibility
- Adaptability
- Accountability
- Consistency

So basically, instead of just mapping out your big game plan the manager is more likely to draft and redraft it. The main idea here is to utilize proper resources to collect and access relevant information. Then use that real-time data to modify your aims and objective. You want to think about how the regulatory challenges are being dealt with. What precautionary measures can you take to overcome them if they reoccur?

The trick here is to adjust your expectations according to the ongoing situation. You might also want to change the game in regards to the marketing trends and customer demands. This helps you have the foresight to understand that even if a strategy worked in the previous year, it might not work in the present one.

Once you accomplish this feat, it will be easier to obtain a clear and accurate picture of where you stand at the end of the year. Additionally, it has been seen that this business strategy helps you to acquire accurate estimates of the expected bottom-line.

Now, all of this might sound too much to digest at first. Odds are that you will be overwhelmed by the sheer amount of information that gets sent your way. It will even take time to process and then act upon the things you learned. However, trust us when we say this business strategy is worth every single penny!

How do you get your whole team on board? This can be done by teaching the fine art of strategic operational alignment.

2. What Is Strategic-Operational Alignment?

Strategic-operational alignment is an effective business strategy that undertakes the task of arranging your strategic priorities in front of the operational realities. This synchronization then helps you prepare and execute your upcoming projects in a better way. Most experts are under the impression that strategic-operational alignment is the best way to secure your short-term goals. Doing so then facilitates their plans to take enable the company's long-term growth.

A textbook definition of this strategy refers to it as the link between the tangible aspects of a company (i.e. structure and resources) with the abstract ones (i.e. values, aims and goals). When you strategically align both extremes of your corporate dynamics, you get a harmonized product. In other words, this business strategy optimizes performances and productivity rates by ensuring that everyone works in a synchronized manner.

How is it different from a business plan? Well, the plan hypothetically places your human resource and predicts how well they will perform. This alignment strategy takes the predicted plan and tries to see if it pulls through in practice. When things don't follow according to the set agenda, the strategic-operational alignment enforces a sense of adaptability.

As a result, you get:

- Measurable outcomes
- Maximize productivity
- Minimal Loss
- Less confusion

On the whole, the strategy helps executives keep all the workers on the same page. This organization proves to be fruitful in generating projects/products that reflect a unified front. In this day and age, the strategy expands its horizons by including the IT department too. This ensures that you aren't misdirected at any certain point due to human error.

3. The Crossroads: How Do You Align Strategies with Operations?

In real life, you can't expect to go anywhere without a sense of direction. So whenever you head out, you equip yourself with a road map that directs you towards your destination. The lack of one will cause you to travel in circles.

In business terms, without a proper plan, you're often left working for a cause that never bears any fruits.

Therefore, strategic-operational alignment comes with a step-by-step guide that ensures your office operates without a hitch.

1. Planning the Perfect Alignment Strategy: What Should You Consider?

The art of perfect alignment is learned by paying close attention to each and every step of your operational process. You've got to identify the checkpoints where a human error or technological glitch is causing a gap in the data flow.

Once you find this problem, your aim is to resolve it in the best way possible.

Do you want to build a purpose-driven corporation?

Of course, you do. That is the ultimate goal of every organization regardless of the industry they work in. The only way to achieve this goal though is to map out a mission. After all, you can't expect to drive your team towards a nameless goal. They need to visualize tangible outcomes and results.

That's why we start off our strategic-operational alignment with a clear-cut vision. You want to create a framework that tries to cover your five-year plans.

Let's look at some of the questions that help you to compose this map:

- What are your long-term goals?
- What are the on-going trends in the industry?
- Who is your target market?
- Do your campaigns meet the requirements of an individual buyer?
- Do you match the expected standards of your industry?
- How do you plan to achieve the set goals?

Apart from this, you want to create a brand persona. It has to be something that creates a brand persona. But in this case, more than appealing the audience, you want your workers to know of the values your company stands for. Let them know of the ethical conditions that shouldn't be crossed. Teach them the general code of conduct that materializes your brand persona.

Overall, this rough sketch helps you to formulate a plan and a mission that pushes the workforce forward. You want them to love the cause they work for and be committed to the future of the company. Your aim at this initial step should be to create a strategy that lays the foundation of everything the company can become with the help of teamwork, devotion and organization. Subsequently, all three factors lead to high-performance and productivity.

2. Filling in the Communication Gaps: How to Keep Everyone in the Loop?

As mentioned earlier in this chapter, you can't expect things to pan out if you isolate yourself to the boardroom. The key to success is hidden beneath the combined effort and transparent communication lines. This is why you must promote and encourage a work culture that believes in openness and sharing.

In the second step of strategic-operation alignment, you will have to sit down with the workers of each department. We suggest that instead of ordering them to work according to your mission, you open lines of communication. The topics and your aspired targets must be discussed by the team.

Ask them to:

- Suggest areas for further improvement
- Bring up concerns and doubts if the need be
- Create their own plans to help reach the set targets
- Inform about any issues that may come up during the operation

Other than the first meetings, you might want to gather the team for weekly/monthly discussions related to the progress. The meetings will help you monitor their progress rates. You will also become of any problems that may have cropped up. Consequently, the timely updates will keep all the team members in the loop. So they will be notified about hold-ups and setbacks in real-time. The transparent method of communication might be the best way to address pending issues or resolve problems in a speedy way.

On the whole, this second phase is all about communication and coordination. The failure to do so might jeopardize your bottom-line productivity. That's because nothing impedes projects like miscommunication, misinterpretation and unwanted office drama.

The Outcomes: Will This Work?

At the end of the day, your primary goal is to get proper outcomes from your team. These outcomes must closely match the strategies you created at the start of a project or business year. Furthermore, you hope to progressively change your organization for the better as you help them meet their deadlines. The only way to turn your visions into reality is by hustling and clear cut plans.

This last phase is incorporates everything you've done so far. The employees expect you to come up with clear strategies when things go wrong and honest opinions at the end of the project. They also need you to stay focused on the future by keeping an eye on everything they do in the present. Now, naturally, you aren't some magic 8 ball that predicts the future.

Nonetheless, a few tricks here and there can help you project substantial results for the company.

The salient features of this phase are to:

- **Data Collection:** You must collect all the important data related to the project. It doesn't matter if whether they are progress charts or performance sheets, the important thing is that you have the data with you. Try to secure all the data from the three phases to help create a more holistic view of your company's performance.

- **Evaluation:** You must now analyze all the data you collected. Compare the strategies with the way they were practically executed. Highlight the things that didn't work out like you imagined and mark the ones that did. You might start to see a pattern that helps you understand the reasons behind the success and failure of certain strategies.

- **Planning:** Use the results of this comparative study to create better strategies for the future. You may also want to pull in team members that had provided useful feedback during phase two. Seek their help to develop functional strategies.

- **Actions:** Remember the weaker areas you found during the evaluation? Your task here is to provide a solution for those problems. This could be anything from training, IT integration, and more communication to outsourcing people. The basic idea is to work on the grey areas to improve your chances of a productive performance in the forthcoming projects.

Once this is done, you can try to sum up the main elements of your next strategic plan. Some businesses try to condense the information on a single sheet of paper. Then they distribute the revised strategic-plan to the whole team. You can either ask employees to send in feedback about the new plans or just keep it as a reminder for new plans. The takeaway message here is to boost employee engagement on the strategically inclined areas of operations. Not only does this give them a heads up on what to expect but they also get a chance to contribute before the project starts.

3. Seeking Help from Technology: Is Software Automation the Answer?

One glance at the strategic alignment process will let you know that it's a lot of hard work. That is why we suggest that you let software automation or rather business process automation (BPA) take over. The integration of IT solutions in your business scheme has been proven to help optimize operations by multifold.

So without further ado, let's find out what software automation is all about:

What is software automation?

Businesses have started to rely more and more on IT solutions. From sending a collective email to your employees to corresponding with the customers —You can do it all with just a click of a button. Therefore, it seems natural to extend the role of IT solutions in your business.

These days, companies have outsourced software agencies to install certain managing tools and apps that can overlook your business. They handle incoming data, process it and then adjust your operational strategies accordingly. The best part here is that they aren't just doing some of the mundane tasks but they're also eliminating the need of a tech specialist to come and deconstruct all the data.

That's because AI technologies come in handy by decoding the unstructured data provides by your analytical team and then implementing it in your operations. You just have to feed it with the right codes and algorithms to get the desired outcomes.

Plus they've got speed, accuracy and lots of data resources on their side.

How does this help your strategic operational alignment?

1. Eliminates Human Errors:

One of the main reasons for delays is human error. Your workers might have punched in the incorrect numbers or send the wrong emails. This can lead to grievous consequences if the project is on a deadline.

Lucky for you, AI assistants rarely make an error. They follow instructions to the T and won't get tired by repeating the same task over and over again. That's why you can trust these smart machines with a bulk order that thrives on consistency and identical execution. This can be relevant to various duties like your bulk marketing emails and analysis of data from customer feedback.

2. Visible Metrics

Your finance and sales departments thrive on numbers. Most of the times your daily collections tend to get overwhelming for a mere human to work on. Whether its sales, billing or data collecting survey, you want a mentally agile mind to be on your time. You know a trustworthy mathematician who can give you accurate statistics in real time.

This is where software automation comes in. They provide you with accurate metrics and reports at a faster pace than a human mind. This ensures that you won't be left waiting around for the statistics just because your sales representative is on a coffee break.

3. *Optimizes Turnovers and Reduces Operational Costs*

How much time goes to waste when you're scrambling for lost files? How many details got lost in the chain emails you sent for the important project?

The answer is one too many. When information gets lost in the rabbit hole of old school communication, there is bound to be delay. You're unintentionally holding up operational lines when you take a precious minute out just to find the missed detail. As a result the turnovers are slow and the deadlines get missed.

Here is where centralized systems come in. Software automation carefully archives each and every detail uploaded on the software. The information is easy to search and won't even take a minute more. Then there is also the fact that the automated processes are almost error-free.

Moreover, you can also use chatbots for customer service. These work really well for the standard customer service procedures where the complaint/query is pretty common. The virtual bot will collect the data required and answer the query accordingly. This gives your sales team the opportunity to attend to other important issues that might crop up in the sales cycle.

Ultimately, you can make the most of your time when you free yourself from these mundane tasks. By letting automation streamline your workflow, you're clearing up your schedule for creativity and innovation.

What about the cost? If you get your calculations straightened out then you'll observe that manual labor costs more than machines. It's all owing to the fact that IT solutions get more work done in less time. Plus, the lack of errors ensures that your operations aren't repeated again.

On the whole, with software automation by your side, you utilize fewer resources and produce more output.

What's the Catch?

We know what you're thinking, 'this sounds good to be true!' Well, it is true and you can really improve your operational turnovers by investing in the BPA software. But like everything else in this world, software automation has some minor setbacks. That's why you shouldn't think of it as a magical bandage that'll fix everything but as an assistant for your operations.

What many companies fail to understand about software automation is that you can't go into it blindly. That'll be like throwing your money down the drain. We say this because; machines aren't as flexible or adaptable as human beings. That is why your error-free codes can't be trusted all the time. Similarly, not every algorithm will be suitable for your business. They might be spouting incorrect numbers because the equation doesn't meet your requirements.

Therefore, you should avoid utilizing configured software that offers standard solutions for bottom-line improvement. This isn't a good tactical move as it frequently creates capital blockages and impedes your workflow due to technical errors. Hence, we feel that this makes large software investments redundant in the long run.

What do you do then? The best way to navigate from this problem is by opting for customized solutions. Therefore, before each purchase, a member of your tech team should conduct a quality assurance procedure. Your main aim here should be to install software that adapts to your business. The rule of the thumb here is to opt for 80% customization. It has to be designed to optimize specific areas of your operations. Doing so helps eliminate any form of ambiguity that may arise if the standard software is unable to work on the task you assigned.

Now, 80% customization here does not mean that we get all your software developed. Rather you should see which of the required apps can actually help you to get a better head start on deployment in comparison to store-bought software.

Sometimes if the software is meets 20% of the organizational needs then that 20% could really become a driving force for your company. It will help you to attain the 80 % in order to complete the successful implementation and deployment for productivity improvement. Under the 80-20 principle it is vital for an organization to adapt according to the resources offered. The rest can be customized to bring about a smoother productive transition.

Even when you get ready-made software, there is always an alternative option. You can ask the IT specialist to install a certain version that can adapt to your unstructured database. Other than that you may get the supplementary products that support your automation. These additional devices should have the capability to give you room for a little customization.

The Bottom Line

In the end, strategic-operational alignment isn't another buzzword that is being tossed around in the business world. Rather it is the necessity for these rapidly changing times. You need to have better control of the operational processes. Or else you'll end up losing more money than you invested in the project. Moreover, shareholders and customers alike prefer to put their money on companies that deliver on time.

This is why we declare that strategic-operational alignment is your winning strategy. So instead of expecting your operations to turn out the way you want. You should be getting down on the operational floor to make collaborative decisions with the team.

Plus, with customized automation software by your side, you get to ensure that each second you spend on the job is directed towards production.

What's more? The next chapter will help you plan for the digitally inclined future. We plan to shed light on all the tech trends and techniques that help maximize output and minimize risks. Let's head on to the digital spaces!

Chapter 6: The Tech Support: Is Technology Your Biggest Asset?

It is an undeniable fact that technology has changed every aspect of how businesses operate in the new millennium. To consider it as your biggest asset is undermining the power of technological advancements for the business world. That's because, in this digital age, technology has rapidly taken over all major sectors of your business. So it isn't *just* an asset but the backbone of your company's future. You can expect it to uplift your profits by a convenient margin and secure further transactions with the utmost ease.

We say this because technologically inclined companies have proven to be leagues ahead of those that are still dependant on conventional methods of operation. And why wouldn't they be?

The latest developments in IT promote productivity, efficiency and improve customer services in a way humanized efforts can't. The boost in your performance rate helps increase customer satisfaction which automatically leads to more popularity and profitability in the market. So it is basically a win-win situation for anyone that is linked to your business.

This chapter will shed light on various areas where adopting IT trends will give you an edge over the competition. Additionally, you might want to understand the benefits and impact of your decision to choose the right technology for your business ventures.

1. How Is Technology Supporting Your Business?

In this virtual age of business marketing and transactions, you can't afford to ignore the various IT developments that have sneaked into the operational and management sectors. One Google search can direct you towards digital solutions that promptly attend to all your business needs. From cashless payments to real-time customer support— we truly live in the golden age of technology!

Here are some of the many ways you can boost your business productivity by utilizing IT solutions for your business problems:

1. Cloud Computing

What is it? Cloud computing is the popular practice amongst businesses that outsource a third-party to host their network of servers. The company's data is stored in a secured place on the internet instead of a personal computer or local server. You are basically utilizing these services to store, process, and manage all the data relevant to your business. In addition to that, the cloud service provider can support your IT needs and problems.

Considering the fact that organization is the key to unlock productivity, this method for organizing and assembling data goes a really long way. Some experts tout it as the hassle-free method of organizing your documents and files. Others point out at the cost benefits of this collaboration because of the lack of equipment involved in the process.

Let's look at some of the many benefits you can avail from this technology:

- **Reduction in IT costs:** IT equipment can cost a fortune and with the frequent updates you might be unable to afford the privilege no matter how important it is. With cloud computing, you keep your company up to date with the latest trends at an economical price. Plus, with no heavy servers or numerous devices operating under your roof, you save a lot on electricity bills too!

- *Flexibility:* Your cloud service provider helps you manage and maintain the software and virtual storage spaces used by the company. Since each project comes with a different set of requirements you have the option of expanding or downsizing your cloud computing package. This helps you accommodate major projects without wasting too much time searching for upgrades.
- *Trustworthy Security:* Cybercrimes are pretty popular in the business world. The dependency on cloud computing helps you to dodge the attacks attempted by hackers and conspirators in the industry. You're able to download, share and use the required data without worrying about a security breach in the system.
- *Reliable Backups:* The unpredictable nature of natural disasters, power failures, and malfunctioning systems make storing data on personal computers risky. Cloud computing provides you with a secure backup option that archives all the data relevant to your business.
- *Portability:* Cloud computing allows you to access data anytime and

anywhere. This allows you to manage the team and projects even when you aren't available in the office. It minimizes the time taken to stay up to date with ongoing businesses during long periods of absence.

More important than all of these factors is the efficient method of organization. The cloud computing method helps you keep tabs on all the operations happening in the company. It also makes accessing information dating a year back really simple. On the whole, this partnership helps you to operate on the same grounds as your biggest competitors. With its assistance, you get access to the best office-based software without spending time or money in getting system upgrades or hardware to support the technology.

2. Mobile Solutions

What is it? It is anything and everything related to smartphones in regards to business interactions. You make use of this facility by distributing the marketing campaigns and contacting collaborators on the small-screened platforms.

The fact that tech giants like Google have rearranged their algorithms to accommodate our mobile habits emphasizes its importance in the business world. The portability factor and popularity has made it easier for companies to reach consumers at all possible hours without invading their privacy.

Technology equips you with a solid selection of media channels that help you reach the target audience. So that now you can say goodbye to the eager salesmen roaming neighborhoods and knocking on doors of prospective buyers. This forum helps you convey your message without annoying the customers.

Why does it work? Your consumers spend countless hours on their phone. Most of the time you see them mindlessly browsing and skimming through information on topics of interest. You can tap into this habit by modifying your methods of communication. From promotional text messages, chat groups to mobile-friendly websites there are countless of open channels that lead us to the consumer. Then if you play your cards right your chosen method of communication can lead to sales.

Apart from this, mobile help you operate and manage business anywhere in the world. This proves to be helpful for executives that travel a lot. Not only does it help them keep tabs on the employees and their activities. But it helps them overlook the meetings and negotiations conducted in their absence. The omnipresent management will help increase the employee's trust in their higher-ups and instills a sense of accountability in the workers.

In short, adopting mobile solutions shows customers and employees alike that you're available to assist them at all times.

3. Extreme Customer Segmentation

What is it? Customer segmentation as the name suggests is a marketing method that divides your customer base into various groups. This segmentation occurs on the basis of each individual's gender, age, consumer preferences and buying habits. Once you have identified the primary groups in your target market, it becomes easier to attend to their needs via your marketing campaigns or customer service.

Why do we do this? You might have heard the saying 'one-size fits-all'. Well, studies show that this is no longer applicable for you sales marketing strategy. In the last few years, the sales or marketing have had a complete makeover as more and more customers are responding to personalized interactions. The main idea here is that your target audience wants to be seen as individuals instead of a broad group.

This is the point where you start getting nervous. How can a team of mere hundreds cater to a market of millions? Even though this might seem possible right now, it's a fairly easy jump if you have the right tools for it. This is where customer segmentation comes in.

The process involves a strategically chosen data collection process that gathers information from various portals. The retrieved information then goes is analyzed and segmented into various customer-based groups. The next phase focuses on detailed discussions regarding the information you've collected over time. Both the sales and marketing teams are supposed to utilize the facts learned for their next campaign.

Apart from this, there is certain software that will automatically feed on this data and then spout our personalized content for each customer.

Here is a list of advantages of this process:

- ***Personalization:*** Your target audience is more receptive to messages when they specifically address them. The customer segmentation strategy helps you do just that by monitoring they're selling habits and acquiring important information via surveys and their browsing activity on your online stores.
- ***Effective Retention:*** When you start to lose customers there is only one way to reel them back in. That is by convincing them that you're the best service and you value them the most. The segmentation strategy helps you retrieve relevant information regarding these customers. You can use that to formulate an effective recovery plan. Additionally, the same data can help you eliminate users that haven't been active in years. This allows you to focus on the main players of your business i.e. the customers who are willing to invest in your business.
- ***Boosts ROI and Marketing Performance:*** Customer segmentation gives you an insight into the sales funnel too. It allows you to recognize the leads from the conversions. This data then helps you to optimize your return-of-investment

rates. The more target-oriented you are in your marketing campaigns the closer you get to make a sale.

- ***Product Segmentation:*** Industry insiders believe that there is more to customer segmentation than shifting your marketing strategies and creating a more direct approach during communication with the customers. You can now use these interests to diversify your company services/products. Use the data you have gathered so far to formulate a new variation for the product you already have. This kind of smart thinking helps you expand your company's prospective customer base.

On the whole, using analytical tools and software is a resourceful way to hit all the right targets. Not only does it help you boost your sales but it provides the customers with a tailor-made experience. Both of these outcomes ensure that the company meets it's projected bottom-line.

What about productivity? Well, think of it this way. The more specific your target audience is the less time you waste chasing after people who will never convert. So basically, customer segmentation is a quick grid search that helps you locate your customers from the crowd of random web users.

That's it!

Invest in these three crucial IT solutions and see your company rise to the top. It can't get any better than that.

2. What Is the Overall Outcome?

We have already explained the tiny improvements that technological advancement brings to your business. You will see the gradual change in your overall performance after a few months of operation. It will take time and patience but equipping yourself with IT solutions is going to take you from point A to Point B at a faster pace.

Nevertheless, there are two benefits that can be witnessed almost immediately. Think of them as the bigger puzzle of this revolutionary picture. You know of its existence but you might not have considered how they really play out in a holistic overview.

So let's have a look:

1. Connectivity:

Time and time again this book has emphasized the importance of communication. But many times messages get lost in translation. You might have said something and the person would have understood something different. Then there is the problem of bringing the team on the same page. Are we right?

This is where various office-specific apps come in handy. They automatically update and synchronize the information on a mutual database. This ensures that your team always stays in the loop no matter how many modifications have been made in the project. Without these links, you are forced to operate as a disintegrated unit that struggles to work in conformity. But with the constant contact, you can coordinate better and influence productivity rates.

So it is all about honing those commutation skills by tuning into technology.

2. Social Impact

The boom of social media networking in customer services provides you with another benefit. It opens an interactive channel to connect with the audience. This form of connectivity proves useful in areas where you need customer insights to improve your sales cycle.

Moreover, the failure to transition into a digitally inclined world reflects poorly on your reputation. That's because to the tech-savvy consumers you'll look outdated and old-fashion. Plus, the non-existential presence on the web might stop you from tracking down industry trends, noticing disgruntled customers and witnessing a change in the demands.

Thus, not including IT as part of your essential operational plan may limit your impact on the targeted customers. This will directly lower your chances of reaching the desired bottom line.

The Bottom Line

On the whole, technology isn't just your biggest asset. Rather it is the only thing that will guarantee a secure future for your company. That is why if you aim to emerge a powerful contender in the business world then you've got empower yourself with technological advancements. Whether they are minute changes like software update or big-scale upgrades like customer segmentation cloud computing and mobile solutions— the basic idea is to always stay on top of the game.

Otherwise, your old-school techniques and archaic filing systems will cause you to lag behind.

So are you ready to embrace the future?

Parting Words

Thank you for investing your precious time to read this book.

We hope that it serves as a guide that helps you find your way through persisting business problems. More importantly, this book was written to help you realize that your bottom line productivity isn't as elusive as it seemed. You can actually meet your targets if you really set your mind to it and grasp that the ever-changing world of corporate management is built on the foundation of proper planning and seamless communication.

We hope that this book proves useful in teaching you how to implement these changes. So that you may learn to streamline operations, optimize productivity and harness the right technology for successful strategic-operational alignment.

So what are you waiting for?

Let's start working for a better and brighter future of your company!

About Ccerebrate Business Consulting

Ccerebrate Business Consulting is one of the leading consultancy firms in India. From startups, mid-level enterprises to established firms— we cater to all of them. All you have to do is book a consultation and we'll be there to lend a hand.

Our team of experts covers every tiny detail of your business framework. You can call us for help during transitional management or ask our advice on core operations. We promise to come through in any kind of business need and in an emergency.

Our aim is to help develop your business plans and strategically organize the corporate structure. With our help, your business ventures will have an edge over the competition. And, that's only the tip of the iceberg for us!

Do you want to know more about who we are? And what we do?

Visit: https://www.cerebratebusinessconsulting.com/

ABOUT THE AUTHOR

Ajatshatru Sharma is the director of Ccerebrate Business Consulting. He has been working in the industry for more than 15 years. His experience and abundant knowledge of industry trends make him one of the best consultants. He is dedicated to directing companies to the right path, which is why he came up with the consulting firm in the first place. He wanted to equip businesses with the right strategies and powerful tips that could boost their performance. From conceptualization to completion - with his advice, you will never miss a deadline or cross the budget. Moreover, he teaches you how to have an imbedded culture that continuously supports and enhances productivity.

"The Secret Guide to Securing the Elusive Bottom Line" is written with a similar goal in mind. Sharma wants to enlighten his readers and show them how streamlining operations, strategical management and teamwork can help achieve greater turnovers.

THE KEY FOCUS OF THE BOOK IS ON:

- Boosting Productivity
- Project Management
- Strategic Operational Alignment
- Adaptation and Integration of Software Automation
  & much more

The book will take you on a journey that goes beyond the norms to catch that slippery bottom line.

www.ingramcontent.com/pod-product-compliance
Lightning Source LLC
Chambersburg PA
CBHW021836170526
45157CB00007B/2817